~ ~ ~

Sunrise

Psalms

Jack Perkins

Dedicated to my life's favorite poem - - Mary Jo

~ ~ ~

·

Published by Moosewood Editions

For additional copies or information please contact
jackperk@mac.com

Sunrise Psalm

Arriving at a gilded moment,
On this sweet Myakka morn,
I see a heron in silhouette
Watching the colors of faith reborn,

And I worry. Can the bird perceive those colors?
Or does he see them as I now see
Him, in colorless monochrome.
What a pity that would be,

To be given a sight but not the sight
To see it and appreciate
The gift and, even more, the Gifter.
On this dilemma I meditate,

But in vain. For back home I discover
That a bird sees colors even better than we.
So with no need to pity, I turn to envy
For what every morning this bird gets to see

While I, only occasionally.
Ah, but I have a blessing conferred
For I get to see not only the sunrise
But also himself, that silhouette bird.

On Poetry

It's not always needed
In writing a poem intended to be
A poem of holy praise
To say Holy.

Rather,
Whisper the hush of breezes through grasses
Reflect the rainbow vibrance of birds
Rehearse their calls, their tremolos
Let be felt the gentle splashing of rain on upturned face

Let creation, seen and felt,
Be the Creator's voice.

Ignition Word

I need a word to ignite this poem alive,
To command like the opening notes of the Beethoven Five.
A word that is sturdy, explosive, bold-faced, mysterious
Surprising the eyes like the flower of a night-blooming cereus.
Touching the punk to the fuse on the Fourth of July.
That's the kind of word needed, so you can see why
I am flummoxed, a fancier of words
Who cannot find the one that will soar with birds,
Hunt with lions, light the rainbow's glow,
Letters concatenated just so
To inflame a magic that tragically I cannot find.
It's there, somewhere, but perversely eluding my mind.
Without it, I cannot write this poem. That's that.
I'm lost for the loss of a G, G, G, E-flat.

Poetry

Is a poem not real poetry if I can see its bones?
If I can discern its framework clean and clear,
Not festooned with tags of sinew and flesh
With which the poet would camouflage the meaning?
Should a poem's lips not be smiling a welcome
Instead of snarling a dare?
Should a poem not invite me in,
A welcomed friend, to be lifted,
Relieved for a moment from the prose of my day?
Is that not what a poem should do,
What a poet should provide?
Frost does it, Dickinson, Berry, Millay, and Browning
Hammerstein, Simon too.
I admire those because they know me.
And because they let me know them.

A poet, to be sure, has to work
If his poem is to work.
It is not simple to craft a poem simple.
But that gives the poet no license to think
That there must be a balance of effort;
That if he works hard the reader should have to work harder;
Extending to me not a gift but a provocation,
Striving to prove himself to be more
By proving me less,
To heighten his standing
By thwarting my understanding.
See how smart I am, he seems to brag,
I can write what you cannot read.

Thoreau said that the works of great poets
(As he seemed to deem himself to be)
Can be understood only by other great poets.
My, doesn't that limit the audience!

Sometimes, I wonder if the poet-obscurantist
Isn't just putting me on.
(Putting on, perhaps, himself as well?)
When I encounter a Gordian knot of lines like:

The hidebound footstool of desecration
Upon which rests the trashman's firmament
Is studded with unguents burning lavender slander
Onto the hides of NASCAR gnats . . . .

I think: Am I a fool being fooled?
And is that indeed the poet's intent?
Does he chortle to know how hard I must labor to find
A meaning he has not included?

What will it take then for me to fashion poems
Open and honest,
Like the children I here would midwife?
Some verses may feel the want of rhyming
Although rhyme be for some as gratuitous
As the shine grocers spray on Red Delicious.

Mere versifying does not a poem make, I understand;
There needs to be wisdom, but it need not be mine.
It may come from the scent of a balsam bough,
From the mists that rise o'er a morning stream;
It can find my ear in a thrush's song
Or glisten with dew on a dogwood leaf.
Those are wisdom enough for my children.
All I need in putting them down,
Is to safeguard their transparency,
That in the end,
The reader can see their bones.

Countryman's Creed

OK. Here is how I got things figgered.
There *is* a God. Says my head not my heart.
Had to be someone or something to get things jiggered
In place where they had to be from the very start.

That's God. But there's somethin' else stirrin' in me
Likin' to move me, steer me which way to go
I reckon that's what they call the Spirit and he
(Or she) is a real good mover-steerer to know.

I believe in him or her. But then there's the other,
That Jesus, the one they call the Holy Son.
I don't know what to think about him, but brother
That dyin' and risin' again? Don't mean to be one

Of those Doubting Thomas guys, but it's hard to believe
That this Jesus came back to life and'll do it again
As they say. Could someone be trying to deceive
Us all? Could *many* be trying? If so, what then?

What to believe? Well, I already said
That I believe God. And doesn't his book make Christ
His son? I'm pretty sure that's what I read.
N'before I got to doubtin', that sufficed.

Now, I sometimes believe and sometimes don't.
At times, I'll take Jesus as holy, at times I won't.
I try, God knows that I try to be a good man,
If I need to do more than that, I'll do what I can,.
As for Jesus, I hope he'll forgive me for doubting still.
Gonna keep workin' on it, promise I will.

Jefferson's Kin

I hear it said by troubled souls
(Who likely don't think themselves troubled souls)
I hear it said: "I get the thing about God
I accept a Holy Spirit moving among us,
Guiding the lucky if not the rest.
I buy all that but still am not sure about --
                                                    Jesus.
I know about him. I've read his reported words
Just as Jefferson did, then excised most,
Concluding that Jesus would never have said them.
Jefferson was not a full believer.
His kin, though, he urged to study and decide for themselves.

Were I a kin of Jefferson, how would I decide?
Or is believing not a decision to be made
But a blessing one either accepts
Or eschews; it's up to the me's, up to the you's.

For me, let the choice be not to suit my friends.
Not dancing to someone else's tune,
I need to hear my own. But who's to play it?
If I believe in a Spirit guiding my life,
A Creator God residing both beyond and within,
Then let them be my orchestra and choir
As I, though still shaded with doubt, declaim
Now I know, I know, I know -- partly.
I believe, I believe, I believe, I believe -- mostly.
Mostly. Not wholly. Not Holy. Not yet.
In this impasse time, my prayer is brief.
God and Spirit, help my unbelief.

Turn Off

Allow me, if you will, to recommend.
That when time comes to head to woods,
You switch electronic gadgets off.
iPad, iPod, iPhone doff.
All connecting consumer goods,
You are better off not to attend

So that nature's voices might speak to you,
Other friends for you to meet
Who have important things to say
That you may listen to today.
Hear them call and sing and tweet;
Listen as they splash and coo.

They know things you won't learn in town
Of woodland life in nature's womb.
Of what goes on within the sea
How blessed the life of a bird can be.
Wonderful moments and beings whom
You'll never meet till you power down.

All Day

All day
God

All day
Inspiriting, indwelling

All day, all night
Always with me,
Always guiding, oft ignored.
He is always with me
But I, not always with Him.
The hassles and habits of living distract,
Interfere;
The superficial
Obscuring the foundational:

I have to stop and get gas
Mustn't forget.
Don't need God for that

Meeting begins at ten
Have to hurry to make it.
Don't need God for that

Wife meets me for lunch
Sharkey's? Blu? Must decide.
Don't need God for that

After lunch, home and quiet time
I could read scripture then
But probably will take a nap;
Don't need God for that.

Afternoon, bills to pay, letters to write
Talk to doctor about my tests.
My tests. Might need God for that

I know it's not right. If God all day is with me
Why do I wait till perceiving a need (Of *mine)*
Before deigning to be with Him?

Why do I feel I don't need God for my living,
But sorely need Him for my life?

On Visiting Dr. Mudd's Cell at Fort Jefferson

How would you like to awake in this seaside resort?
A wall on a sea of a never-seen blue
Spray-men standing for just a moment
Atop the brick wall, posing to topple,
New spray-men leaping to take their place

How would you like to awake to slurps and spatters
Through the windowless window of your room
As here today you sit.
As yesterday you here you sat
As day before here you sat
As tomorrow and every of your tomorrows to come
Here you will sit;
How would you like?

Could you tolerate incessant beauty
Taunting and teasing you every hour
With knowing that the sea out there is free
While the wall marks your moat of futility;

Mortared stacks, sixteen million bricks
Brought here torturously years ago
Now to torture you
In this nowhere paradise
Become your *onlywhere*.

Your Life

Someone put pictures of you on a board,
The board on an easel, the table draped black
Collage of your medals arrayed in a frame.

That was your life.

Many were invited; of those who could afford
The time and travel, here and back
It was nice how many came.

For your life.

As last I'd seen you, you wouldn't have known
What was happening or who they were
But, of course this day was not for you

But them.

They wanted, perhaps, to come and atone
For the times they ignored you. Many would prefer
To forget how for years you died out of view.

That was your dying.

Those must have been most trying days
And nights. More than you let people know.
But you knew, didn't you? You knew your lot.

The end to come.

Funeral finished, friends go their ways.
Wanna have dinner? Sure, let's go.
Some for a while will weep,
Till tears dilute the memories,
Wash them away,
And you are, once more, forgot.

That was your life.

Bobby Igoe

Bobby Igoe! Why did that name just erupt
In my mind? It's morning; I'm driving out to the woods
Thinking of woods, when -- flash -- that name
Invades my thoughts unbidden, unwanted.

Bobby Igoe. Face from a high school yearbook
Long since moldered away. But here's that name
Insisting I remember what I long since forgot.
Why put me through this testing, O capricious mind?

Bobby Igoe. I let the name go years ago
And I moved on and so, I imagine, did he.
I never really knew him anyway
Just the name, fun for school kids to mock

Bobby Igoe. Now the name mocks *me*
Denying me this morning the solace of the woods
Fixing my mind instead on my mind itself,
Poisonous, unyielding introspection.

Bobby Igoe. Is memory like a hard drive?
Strictly limited capacity?
Are there only so many names I have room to remember?
When a new name appears am I bound to lose an old?

Bobby Igoe. Who, then, has he supplanted?
My old speech coach? No. Bob Pollock, I remember.
First News Director? Charlie Day. He's still there.
Scoutmaster, Troop 61? Uh-oh. Damn! He's gone.

Bobby Igoe has taken his place on the drive. That's wrong.
Just wrong. But I guess that's how the mind works.
And didn't Bobby have a younger brother?
What was his name? Tommy? Billy? Jim!

Jimmy Igoe. Now, I remember him too.
No! I don't want to remember him.
If I have reinstalled Jimmy Igoe
Into my memory drive, whom, *now*, have I lost?
Go.
You go,
Igoes.

Bo Tree

It was such a tree Siddhartha sat beneath
For weeks that must have seemed like years
In pensive reflection, pursuing the wonder
Of which his life was in sore arrears

Raised in a family of wealth he had found
That that way of living would not lead
To grace or what he called *Nirvana*
Nor would asceticism. Then what indeed?

Simple truths, unsimple to know
Not found in excess, nor in privation
Neither gluttony nor starvation
But a Middle Way he would formulate.
Four Truths he would articulate
As the Buddha pondered 'neath the Bo.

We know there are still many trees called Bo
But Buddha, of him, too few know.

Rolling Fence

I know what Robert Frost believed
About the love of a wall.
I, on the other hand to him and you would say --

Something there is that dearly loves a fence
Surfing grassy waves beside a mountain road
Railing trailing toward infinity
Teasing me to see what I will not see
But will enjoy the quest as I
Roll by a rolling fence that does not move
But transports me.

Corinth

We find ourselves living in Corinth these days
As Corinth was in those days,
Drunken, lewd, incestuous profaners,
Worshiping any god
Worshiping many gods
Or worshipping only themselves;
Believing that right is whatever they say it to be
And that really there is no wrong.
That was how they of old believed and behaved.
Now old is new.
History cycles but does not change.

Would that we had us a Changer like Paul
To set into changing our Corinth today.
He never fully accomplished back then,
No, but he tried,
By God, he tried.
Who is trying today?

Of course, there are many. Many try.
But I?
Could it be
That the mantle of Paul
Is meant as well for me?
Surely not me, this late in life.

I had a chance.
Many times I had a chance.
If in my parents' home the Bible remained unopened,
At least there was a Bible;
If occasional churching was social
Not spiritual
Still there was church.
I had a chance.

If later I came to select a church
For the appeal of a pastor
Why was that all?
Why did I get familiar with churches, church people
And still not learn to know
Truly, intimately, deeply,
Him whose house I was in?
Until now, so late?
So late.
What took me?

I am just one man, aging and frail
Surely not fit to inhabit the mantle of Paul.
Where would I get the strength?

Where did he?

Flying / Flown

Through a river of light, tiny somethings swim,
Specks being propelled away from me.
I see their stream of light but little else;
The rest of the cabin is dark. Most passengers
Having pulled their shades to watch a film.
(Fliers like to distract themselves from flying.)
One window, though, glares bright across the aisle
And through it the brilliance of morning pours
Creating the stream in which the specks seem to swim.

Ah, but there's something contradictory.
For the light is streaming toward me; the swimmers away.
I ponder, fist to mouth, the Rodin pose.
One sharp exhalation and I am brought
To understand more than I wish to understand;
To identify those sunlit, swimming specks.

They are I.
Minuscule flecks of me fleeing me.
Flakes from my hand escaping in the stream.
Ever to be replaced?
I must assume,
Else, by the end of this flight,

                                        I may have flown.

Isaac and Johnny

Of a sudden, the plane begins to heave and yaw,
Passengers' jaws and hands on armrests clench.
We fly in anxious uncertainty. Why?
Comes a p.a. voice to explain and quench

The fears. *We're experiencing some turbulence.*
We're flying directly over hurricane.
Isaac. The storm that's pummeling the gulf
Thirty thousand feet below our plane.

People down there hurting, dying? — while we
Up here are merely jounced for half an hour,
Thanks to a machine that rises above the storms.
It's good, I reflect, to have a higher power.

And at that moment, coincidence, unplanned.
A Johnny Cash track begins to play
In my ears. He, a man about to meet
His own Higher Power when one near-dying day

He expended penultimate breaths reminding me
On this bucketing 737 today to try
To rethink my life as he did his. He sings:

I came to believe in a power much higher than I.
I came to believe that I needed help to get by
In childlike faith I gave in and gave Him a try
And I came to believe in a power much higher than I.

The air at our altitude calming, on we fly.

Perspective I

Do you find yourself sometimes jealous a bit?
You're on an airplane, peering obliquely out
Through a porthole, scratched,
At the fortunate folk down there in the heart
Of nature's majesty,
God's gifted glory,
While you, alas, are cocooned and bound
Up here?

Or . . .

Do you find yourself sometimes jealous a bit
To look up, squinting into the burning sun-sky
At the contrail of travelers aloft?
They see it all, up there, surveying the spread
Of nature's majesty,
God's gifted glory,
While you, alas, are wingless and bound
Down here.

Perspective II

Cow in the field, one side of the wire;
On the other a photographer.
Between them, a question.

You there, animal I see,
Why are you standing there staring at me?
Who are you?
Are you bound somewhere?
If so, whither, whence?
Or are you, as I, simply bound by this fence?
Meant, I guess, to keep one of us in
And one of us out.
Why?
Why would anyone want to keep you
And your camera out?

Wonder

What has happened to wonder, I wonder?
Do we have no more room in our lives for awe?
Does the puffy quilt of the sky we are under
No longer inspire us to draw

A thankful breath of admiration?
Have we gullibles grown so numb,
To the bountiful feast of all creation
That we have finally become

Persuaded that knowing all we need
To know, we no longer need to believe.
That knowledge trumps wishfulness, guaranteed.
If that's how we think, we are so naive.

We can map the heavens, that we can do,
But does that mean that Heaven does not exist?
We know the sky is not really blue,
But in my mind blue skies persist.

Movement of planets, depth of sea,
Atoms, Big Bang, Warming, it'll
Drive us mad, the perplexity
Of knowing so much while believing so little.

I think of the knowers knowing their way,
The believers believing their replies.
And I think no wonder there's no wonder today;
Too many of us are too smart to be wise.

Joe

We departed the home of our hearts some years back.
Left the cabin, the woods and the trails.
The apple trees, the lilac stand,
The memories and expectations. Abandoned those,
And the crows.

Intimate had been our lives with crows on the island.
Admiring them and faithfully letting them know we admired
The iridescent sheen of feather,
Cleverness of mind. The wisdom of the birds.
We never had reason to doubt the books
That put crows among the smartest of species.
Ours were. (And, yes, we arrogated them as "ours"
And hoped they thought of us as "theirs.")

If we had spaghetti for dinner
Their scout could spy through the window and pass the word
So his fellows knew to be alert next morning,
Gathered up the path for the waited moment.
A call from the woman would bring them flying
To the leftover pasta spread across their table path
Soon we would be enjoying the peculiar scene:
Stately black birds proudly displaying
Their drooping noodle mustaches.
(Grateful we used spaghetti,
Not farfalle or radiatori.)

None of those crows, best we know, was named Joe.
But there was a Joe Crow who wangled into our lives.
Gunshot in the wing, unable to fly,
Rescued by a Ranger who thought of us,
Us, the Crow Folk as word abroad had it.
So our cabin became Recovery Room for Joe,
Confined in a cage for six weeks,
Transferred to a larger cage
(We used to call it our dining room) another six weeks.
At each end of day, when roosting time came for communal
crows,
Joe fretted and fussed each eve on his internment perch
Until finally time and rest had healed him
Joe was ready to be free.

Magic, it was.
Magic, the moment he realized that the door beside his roost
Had been opened and remained.
Warily, down to the floor he hopped,
Over to the beckoning door, tentative,
Looking this way, that, then stepping out.
And in seconds, a swooping sweep of crows surrounded,
Shoulder to shoulder encouraging, guiding
Their brother onto a low branch near
Then up to a next and another, Joe hopping his way to near the top,
Resting a moment, and then the whole murder taking flight,
Away.

Next day, too briefly, we saw him once more.
Looping past our now again dining room door,
With slightly drooping wing,
Passing by, then passing on.
That final sighting, we took as his goodbye and thanks.

Farewell, Joe.

Now, these years later,
We return to the home of our hearts.
Not to the cabin, long since bulldozed.
This day, in its stead, bright summer grasses overgrow.
Nature reclaims. No memory of us remains.
Except --
Here come crows.
(How terrible to call them a "murder.")
Crows flying, settling, walking about,
Then one of them warily walking straight toward us.
Could it be?

Crows live twenty years. This is ten.

Hello, Joe?

The Road That Winds to Woods

It wends and winds through daisy-freckled field
To find the woods and disappear;
And where from there?
Those who do not know
Receive no absolution from the puddled, island road.

But I its secrets share
And, sharing, am renewed.
The jangles of the day are calmed,
Its toxins laved away,
Its vexing, pressing problems
Fade with fading day.
It's time, at last, to bid the afternoon a sweet *Shalom*
And walk the road that winds to woods --
The road that takes me home.

City Seasons

If you must, but only if you must
You can endure the winter in a city
If you'll adjust your expectations
To snow too quickly gray and gritty,
To businessmen all in the same clothiers plaid
Scurrying the avenue they aptly call Mad.

Spring in the city is easily missed.
Most citians never see spring flowers
Except the plastic potted bouquets
Going gritty in city bowers.

Summer in a city can be borne
Sweating streets that bleating taxis drive
All who can escape, escape
While worker bees stay back in the hive.

Summer, spring, winter, okay,
A city can barely be endured,
But in autumn, in autumn, you must get away.
Must let yourself to woods be lured.

Fall Fall

First come showers, gentle but steady
Loosening holds of leaves to their branches.
Then, showers subsiding, autumn breezes
Whisking and teasing high in the trees
Catching first the most vulnerable leaves.
Until soon . . .

Soon the falling of fall is begun,
The fluttering, flittering, skittering, scattering,
Showering again but now, showers of butterflies,
Multifold dazzles of dancing butterflies
Not aimless flutters but choreographed,
Each seemingly wayward descending leaf, terpsichorean.
Here, a maple leaf *tour jeté,*
There, a red oak leaf *plié ,*
An *arabesque,* an *entrechat,*
Mostly the movements trending downward
But now and then a gust lifts the dancers
To begin their descending ballet once more,
Their delicate dance of dying defied.

Brilliant performance if played to a limited crowd.
(Devoted artists, though, we're told,
Perform not for audience but art.)
Art it is today, perhaps as well
A sequel tomorrow, maybe the next, the next,
Then closes the show for this Fall Fall.
But before you leave today be sure to book
Your tickets to be back right here
Next year.

Snowbirds

Some
When winters come
Collect their things and head
With birds to warmer climes instead.
To Florida, perhaps, they pack and go
To any place likely to know --*No Snow!*

No snow in which proud birches take their winter stance
Across whose bosom sparkle-fairies dance
No white-on-white of shadow play
For those who've gone away
To sun-warmed city.

Pity!

Snowflake

How fragile the snowflake --

A touch,
        A breath,
                It's gone

Has nature ever made a thing more tenuous,
More tender?

And yet think again next you find yourself
Out in winter weather
Of all the things those fragile flakes can do
When they stick together

Floaters

Like floaters in my eye beheld
Are thought-flecks in my mind
Floating as though unattached, uncommitted.
Fixed to nothing,
Drifting as though aimlessly.
I see them there but do not dare
To *try* to see them
For rolling my eye to focus on them
Makes them flee and hide,
Leaving me to wonder
How did those that just were here
With only a twitch, disappear?
And how dare they? Those flecks were precious thoughts
Unborn. Aborted before fully formed.
Shall I never find them again?

I guess the lesson is to treasure floaters,
Encourage them to stay, floating free
To be what they are
And become what they will.
Just don't expect to fix them in my gaze.
Ideas, like eye-flecks, are hard to pin down.

Ironies

Paying bills in my office this morning,
Reaching for the Pest Control invoice,
From the envelope wriggles a silverfish.

I love life's little ironies

Full Moon Seen Atop A Cactus

When the desert moon becomes a lollipop,
When angels waltz on the head of a pin,
When red means go and green says stop,
Will I remember?

When I drive on a parkway and park in a drive,
When I hear that Munch has painted a grin
When bees forget where they put the hive
I think I'll remember.

When desert shivers; Arctic sweats,
When Vegas decides to give up sin
And pay off every single bet,
I'm sure I'll remember.

When the mockingbird can't remember a tune,
When the Captain of Mensa flunks a quiz,
When a lollipop becomes the moon --
Wait!
       I remember.
              It *is*.

Progress' Pilgrims

The scene is simple and serene,
But something is missing, something seen
Many times but not today.
The sandhill cranes have gone away
From their home; their fields and woods now overrun
By grumbling machines, their devouring begun.

When cranes take over, cranes take wing,
As offstage someone starts to sing
A rousing verse of the Progress Song,
A verse that says there's nothing wrong
With mankind being less than kind
To species otherwise defined,
If their ways tend to interfere
With what mankind has plotted here.

It's Man's dominion, Bible-blessed;
Genesis should put to rest
Any niggling, nagging qualms
As iron jaws devour palms
And what are classed as nuisance trees
(By nuisances who write decrees.)
So now, where red-head Sandhills stood
Secure at the edge of the unspoiled wood
Machines begin to spoil all
So the world can have — another mall.

*PS. A critic friend who often complains
Complains those machines would not have been cranes.
Perhaps, sir.
But the birds were.*

Time

Think it the scoop with which our lives are portioned,
Micrometer of moments, ruler of days
(Using "Ruler" in either of two definitions
Ruler: the monarch who dictates our days and our ways,

Or ruler which measures them.) Monarch or yardstick,
Both apply on this merry-go-round that I'm
To ride in ceaseless pursuit of a life always
Ruled and dictated, measured and portioned -- by *time*.

Time. At times we don't feel we have enough
At times, anxiously waiting, we have too much.
Time. Times. We label our highs and our lows
Good Times, Bad Times, Painful Times or such

But so naming we miss a point. Time is
Never in itself painful or good or bad
What we did with our time, used or misused,
Is that which gave us the kind of Times we had.

Time is God's most bewildering enigma
Time *was* but *isn't*; time *is* but *will not be*.
It's widely believed a person should live in the *now*
But how, when the *now* is already history?

As for the past, why worry now? It's gone.
And the future? The future is destiny
I don't know mine but I will not fret for the future
For the future for me might never be. I'll see,
In time.

In time.

In time.

Revelation

O, woman of faltering faith,
O, Man too wise to believe,
You who have room in yourselves
For naught but yourselves,
It is you to whom it is spoken,
It is you the surrounding mountains address,
You in the lowlands, they from their peaks
Asking:

Did you make us?
Did you mold us from Creation Clay?
Set us to tower o'er field and plain?
Send waters to fill the banks of winding rivers and streams?
Make them the hope that would nourish thirsty dreams?
Did you do that?

Look up.
Can you even comprehend how far you see?
And how far beyond that you cannot?
If you cannot these comprehend,
You surely did not create.

So you come to your hardest question
(Though it's only hard if you let it be posed;
Ignore it, do a Doubter's Dance around it
And you will find it is not hard at all.
Questions unasked never are.)

Ask it, make yourself ask it,
And as you do, a dazzling door,
A portal of fire will appear before you,
Resplendent and frightening.
Fear it not.
Swing it open and find the damning dazzle
Transformed to a beckoning radiance.
It has heard your question
And offers as reply this revelation.

O, woman of faltering faith,
O, Man too wise to believe,
You who have room in yourselves
For naught but yourselves,
You know you did not build the mountains;
Nor cause the nourishing waters to flow;
You cannot measure or even conceive the vastnesses
Surrounding your minuscule, negligible selves,
But be assured by the flames of ultimate truth
That to Him who did build and flow and conceive,
You are not minuscule if you are in Him.
You are negligible only neglecting Him.

Sentinel, Was

Brightly luminous skeleton tree
Standing against the dark of the living
Trying to remember what it was
When it was.

They called it evergreen.
How wrong they were.
Long as it could it stood as sentinel, outlier
Mostly alone but for the birds it welcomed.
They were glad it was here for a while.
Now they, too, have forsaken
The luminous tree which somehow persists,
An outlier still,
Sentinel no more.

Reaching

One spring in the meadow, one long ago year
Sap would not pulse through the apple tree's core,
Nor vernal buds of leaf appear,
Nor sweetening blossoms; never more
Would romping child or browsing deer
Savor the fruit of its long ago store.

Yet still it would stand, that derelict tree
Survivor no longer surviving, yet each
Passing season here it would be
Fingering upward as though to reach
To the Maker of trees, the Maker of me.

What a lesson that patient tree has been teaching.
I pray, my time come, I too will be
Still reaching, still reaching.

Dim / Glare

Fear not the dark,
The shadowed and dim

Let them not chase you off to brightness,
To brilliance.
Beware of those.
Dazzle distracts,
Effulgence seduces,
Truth is not found in glare.

In the Dim

When the sun doesn't shine,
When the day breaks gray
A storm just passed
Or a storm on the way
God, in that dim,
Is closest to me;

I, to Him.

Thirteen

Today is given the number thirteen;
Thirteen, too, is the year.
I worry not about any of that.
From the curse called *triskaidekaphobia*
I am more than immune.

For me, that "curse" is an everlifting joy.
Call me a *triskaidekaphile*.
Whose wife was born on a Friday thirteen.
No better fortune know I.

Morning Chores

The checkbook is here by the bed as I wake;
The Do-List lies on the table beside.
The alarm clock an insistent reminder:
I must be up and about the chores assigned
To me, by me and no delay.

Dawn-colors already light the east
Beyond the bay. Birds will soon call.
They also have Do-Lists to attend
Theirs, more urgent, more living-dependent.
They must provision for themselves
And those dependent on them.

So, in a more indirect way, must I.
They and I, I'm assured, are looked after by the Maker.
But only, while able, we do our morning chores.

Bison bison bison

The original American,
Mighty monarch of the plains
Who used to range in myriads
Of which but memory remains.

Today, to guarantee all eyes,
All minds, all focus be on him
The over-towering mountains deign
To shroud themselves behind a scrim

That he alone, in ragged robe,
Shakespearean, commands the stage,
Soliloquizing in the mist,
This icon of another age.

Buffalo, some people say
Who haven't checked the formal list.
For Bison bison bison decreed
A stammering taxonomist

A treble name to comprehend
This ponderous ton of antiquity
Yielder of meat, provider of warmth,
And occasional iniquity.

This greatest beast is more to be feared
By man than wolf or cat or bear
And yet, and yet, something happens this day.
I think it happens. Allow me to share:

I step from behind the camera and climb
The grass of his hill, an exercise
That brings me gazing into his gaze,
Those knowing orbs, those ancient eyes.

Grasping his horns I slowly lower
My forehead to his; he does not stir.
Neither of us is surprised as it happens,
Cool skin cleaving to his warm fur

The steam of his breathing moistens my face
I inhale the damp and close my eyes
Close my eyes but still can see,
Though not as before, and I realize

No longer am I without, gazing in,
But somehow I am within seeing out,
Seeing as he sees. How can that be?
I don't understand, but do not doubt.

I sense in my sinews a confounding truth
That a transformation has begun:
Now I am he, looking down and seeing me:
And we are kin, and we are one.

I raise my gaze to a milky sky
That has no shape or form or face
And yet I know it, know that from it
Somehow I feel comfort. Place

Me on my hill or in a meadow,
Or out across the plain and I
Will always be connected to
The power of that milky sky.
It gives me freedom, finds me grass,
Gives me all I know as real.
I guess it even provides this very
Curious feeling that I feel.

But wait. No longer cool skin against my fur
That's not what I'm feeling now.
I'm feeling -- How strange, and yet how familiar! --
I'm feeling warm fur beneath my brow.

Releasing the horns, I raise my head
And there again are those ancient eyes.
Ponderous One and ponderer,
Each the other in disguise.

Or am I daft? Was it all chimera?
Transmigration cannot be.
Still, I stick to my story. After all, a group
Of us bison is called an Obstinacy.

Petaled

They and their calendar say it's spring;
I'll take their word
Although for me it won't be spring until

I hear an unseen meadowlark
Begin to sing
Of her availability

See the scamper
Of diminutive beings
Emerging from burrows of meadow grass

Taste the nectar that drips
From the cut I slice
In maple bark or birch

Scent the perfume
Of lilacs along the lane
Recalling the past

Or, lying beneath a flowering apple
And closing my eyes,
I feel my face being petaled upon.

What Is A Boy?

The Bible tells how
      Years and years,
      And years and years,
      And years and years ago
God created Man and Woman

What the Bible does not tell
      But yet we know
Is how every day,
      Today,
      The day before,
      The day and days to come,
God creates his sweetest and most precious gift of all —
      The Child.
Children come in different colors, different sizes,
But the basic distinction is this:

Some of those children are girls
Some of those children are boys
      And, oh, what a difference it makes!

What is a Boy?

A boy is a bundle of spirit and spunk
All the mischief of the cosmos sparkles in his eyes.

He is noise
      Raucous when right
          (Or thinking he's right)
      Mumbles and grumbles when knowing he's wrong

He is energy, restless, always moving
      Unless you want him to move
Because -- the first of his many contradictions —
He is also inertia, unwilling to change:
      If in bed, he wants to stay in bed
      If up, he wants to stay up
Contrary, you may call him
  I call him, simply, Boy.

Boys, today, are not what they used to be; times are not what
they were
      Today, Huck Finn has a Game Boy
      Tom Sawyer, an MP3

But still they thrill to rafts on a river
>Or conning someone else to paint the fence.

Some things don't change
>>A boy can still lie on the grass and see faces in clouds
>>>And horses
>>>And dragons
>>>And monsters
>>>And Grandma's bent-over rump
>>He still can skip stones on calm-water ponds
>>Still loves a tree to climb.

Other things a boy loves:

Things that fly
>Kites
>Planes
>Birds (at least big ones like eagles)
>Sometimes he dreams that he too,
>>If only he really believed
>>>Could fly
>>>(You, too, think maybe he could
>>>>But hope he won't try)

Camping
Riding his bike or his buzz-motor scooter
Wearing jeans with holes and baggy T's
>(*Why can't I wear 'em to church?*)
Picking on little brothers
Teasing little girls
>No use trying to tell him he'll ever feel different.
>>A boy wants to believe that girls will always
be there
>>>To tease

A boy also loves

>Having fun
>Being funny
>>(Though of course, a boy's idea of funny
>>Is funny only to boys
>>>If grownups
>>>>a. Don't get boys' humor,
>>>or
>>>>b. b. Think it's gross and
>>>>disgusting
>>>*Then that's the funniest of all*

**Those are things a boy loves. But here are more important
things than those. Things a boy needs:**

Secrets.

      They don't have to be important. It's fine if they're not. Just as long as they're secret.

            Especially from you.

A dog.

      Not a sissy dog, all frou-frou and ribbons.

            To a boy, a dog with ribbons might as well be a cat

                A girl might do with a cat or a bunny or bird

                But a boy must have a dog.

            To get it he'll promise earnestly to

                Take care of it

                Feed it

                Clean up for it

                    And he will.

                        For a day.

            After that, the job will fall to someone else

          while he does the most important work

      Loving his dog

      Romping with it

      Chasing it

            Letting it chase him

            Playing ball with it till he tires

            (The dog never will)

      And begging you to let it sleep on his bed.

            Which you won't

                But it will

And that's really okay

      You let a boy's dog get special treatment because

            Even more than he loves his dog

                You love him.

Other things a boy loves:

From his earliest crawling-around days, a boy loves cars.

            Cars he can push on the floor

             Cars he can see on the street

             Cars he can come to name and know

             Cars that, one day

                Long *before* you're ready

                Long *after* he thinks he is

             He finally can drive.

That's one of a boy's greatest urgings –

            The permit

            The license

            To drive

He never outgrows it
And if you think a boy loves cars —
      He absolutely, most of all, loves trucks!
Cars go *hrummmmmmmmmmm*
Trucks go HRUMMMMMMMMMMM!!!!!!
          And bigger and louder, for a boy, are best
        Trucks haul things; trucks work; trucks are tough.
        Like boys
          That's what boys believe
          It's important to a boy – to be tough
            To be thought of as tough
            Even if *he* doesn't think he is tough
              He wants *you* to
And here, one more contradiction
        While wanting you to think he is tough
        He also, when he needs it, wants you to
        Feel sorry for him
          To care for him
          To hold him
        A boy may pretend that he doesn't like to be hugged
but that's just being a boy.
          He *does* like to be hugged. Truly.
            Not kissed, perhaps, at least not in
   sight of his friends
          But hugged
            An embracing, reassuring hug he
can   only get from you.

It's with you, parents, that a boy has his toughest time
      He is changing; he wishes *you* would
      You are secure; *he* would like to be

A boy won't tell you
      He won't really know
        And you won't guess from how he acts
But he really does want to grow up like you
      It's just that first he has to try to be the opposite
        To love music you hate
        To dress some other way
        To invent his own manners and style
          As he tries to become himself
            By being the anti-you

He'll learn.
   Eventually, after trying other ways, he'll learn
      And come back
      And when finally he does
        The sweetest thing is:

He will think it is *you* who have changed.

He'll be happily surprised by how much you
have learned
And assume you learned it, somehow,
from him.

That is a Boy
Teaser, tough guy, urchin, imp
Soiled and spoiled.

Child of yours
Child of God
Loved by you,
Loved by God,
Who will grow and go
But however grown
However gone
To you,
He will always be
Your Boy

New Moon

I'm wondering if this day will bring me joy or trial
When up in the ink black sky breaks either a smile,
Or the rim of a teacup sharply carved in the night,
Beginning softly to pour its liquid light
Out across the waters of the sea,
A luminous runner rolled out to welcome me
Into approaching day and into the smile.
I sip a cup of grace, as all the while
I am lifted by the word of a nearby bird.
It's a bird called a screech but it was no screech I heard
From that unseen owl. His call was more a coo,
A coo that smiled and made me smile too.

The moon, the sea, the owl, that sound of his --
Is it going to be a good day?
                              It already is!

Come Sit With Me

Come sit with me at sunrise.
Help me say "Good morning, Morning,"
Greet the hatching day.
When sun is not yet seen but known
By muted hues of promise that live this time alone,
When it's no longer dark but not yet light,
When it's not yet day but will be soon.

Sit with me at sunrise.
We know the secret of this hour,
That earth is turning, sun stands still,
And so it's not the sun that soon will rise but we.

It's now we need to be together,
You and I and God. Our private Trinity.
Throughout this rising day we may face odds,
That we cannot foresee.
But whatever those odds,
We know if God is with us,
We're a majority.

Old Boards

Old boards bend and tend to shrink,
Buildings sag and, sighing, settle.
Does that mean we should only think
Of how they were in better fettle,
Pretending no change do we observe?
That does them no honor; they may be robust
No longer, but proud and willing to serve
Until their time of dust to dust.

Old Bones

Old bones bend and tend to shrink,
Bodies sag and, sighing, settle . . .

Four Voices

The Emperor Napoleon said it plain:
"I know men and I tell you, Jesus is more than a man."

Ralph Waldo Emerson, more succinct:
"Jesus was not just a man."

Arnold Toynbee, scanning time:
"...Eyes fixed upon the farther shore,
A simple figure rises from the flood
And straightway fills history's horizon.
There is the savior."

Emperor, Poet-Philosopher, Historian.
And who brought those of witness together
For me to consider this day?
No less than Billy Graham.

I gladly sing with that quartet.

All

A voice unseen speaks to me at the beach.

Look to the empty; discover the void
Nothing to see but sea and sky
No need for you to be annoyed
For these themselves are bequests that I
Created for you days three and four --
Before you were, and forever more.

So see the sea and see the sky
Adorned with clouds to glorify
While light makes bright their blooms of white
And shadows among them imitate night
Occluding my face from out your sight.
But you need not see the Holy Face
To know I am within a place.
I offer signs to son and daughter:
My joy in their faithfulness sparkles the water;
To them I shall cling through all their trials
While those prophets who profit from damning denials
They shall be damned to eternity.

Look then again at the spread of the sea
Gaze on it acknowledging
That from less than this came everything
By accident? What insolence!
My name is not Coincidence!
Call me Creator of great and small
*Call me -- call me simply -- **ALL**!*

Hallowed / Hollowed

In everything I do today
Hallowed be thy name.
In all I write and all I say
Hallowed be thy name.
Sun or rain; peace or pain
Hallowed be thy name.
Spending, earning; teaching, learning
Hallowed be thy name.

Hallowed be you; as *hollowed* be I
Emptied of all of my plans and pride
Leaving welcoming space inside
Of me for you to occupy

And begin transforming. Let it be.
Carry on the work you have begun,
You and the Spirit and Holy Son.
Hallowed be you all -- in hollowed me.

The South

Sultry, they say, is the South.
Live oak dripping sunlit syrup moss,
Voices dripping *y'alls* and *Suh's,*
The sorghum-slurred speech of the South.
Biscuits steam in the heat of the South
Which, in turn, makes butter melt better
And the sorghum taste real sweet.
Some people complain that folks
Don't move so fast in the South,
Maybe that's 'cause they're content where they are.

Primary Color

My love is a primary color.
Not a secondary
Not a color compounded of others;
But pure, extraordinary.

She is not shy, my primary
Color, but proudly displayed;
A hue that is always true
Unbesmirched, not darkened a shade.

Nor is she diluted,
Faded to a tint
No, my primary color,
Is a statement, not merely a hint.

She may behave pastel
When that can help dispel
The heat and hate that oft abound
Amid the clashing of colors and sound;
For that, she may subdue her tone
While inside, remaining her own
Primary color, always true,
Her authentic, God-given hue.

Words

Our lives are colorful tapestries woven of words
Words spoken, words read, words heard,
Words remembered, forgot.
Words prolix, discursive, verbose, (like this very line),
Logorrheic weavings of warp and weft.
Such are our lives. From the very start and still.

Curious, then, to find that the very word "still"
Counteracts, countermands all of the words above.
Stillness quells speech, obviates verbiage,
Does not preclude meaning however. Most meaningful,
Most powerful are meanings that need no words.
Stillness declaims wordlessly.

Shhhhhhh!

Talking

When, as babes, we started talking
Long before we learned to speak
It was prattles and chatter and hollow twaddle
That we thought O so eloquent.
Early, we started believing that we
Had insights that must be given,
Unsolicited to all
In sight or imagined.
We possessed, we were certain, wisdom
And life-sparking insights, as yet unsentenced.
So we tried and tried to talk and
Over years, spent so much time learning to talk
And talking
We had little time left to listen.

Looking back, I would say that for me,
Over years,
Talking often did in hearing.

Why I Don't Answer

And where is that?
The photograph hangs on a gallery wall
A man, perusing, feels need to know
Where is that?

"Hanging on the wall," I say
Too curt I know but why say more?
I figure no longer is it just a picture
A simple stalk, waxing moon, amped up blue of sky
It is now -- or I esteem it to be – a work of art
Hanging on the wall

Another viewer, viewing
A geometric tangle of Spanish moss-draped
Live-oak trees. inquires

Is that your picture?
"Yes, ma'am, I say,"
And where is that?

I mellow: "Cumberland Island," I say
And she responds
Oh, I love Cumberland Island.
Have you ever been there?

That's why I don't answer anymore.

Pity

I pity those

    With tongues too often untethered to minds
    Who presume their sainthood
       by damning others as sinners
    Who loll when they could be achieving
    Who are shiftless or, worse, shifty
    Who, with others around, see only themselves
       Content in the dark of their own illumination

What does my pitying all these accomplish?

It lets me feel superior
                        Isn't that what pity is for?

Wind

I do not know the wind. Have never seen it
Know not whence it comes nor whither goes.
I can hear it; at times, can feel it,
Still know it not. Only that it blows,

Sometimes gentled as a breeze to brush
My face, caressing my awareness.
Soft, it is, and softly received, and then is gone.
Eastward? Westward? Somehow raised aloft?

I'm not to know. The wind, you see, is a spirit.
The Greek word for *spirit*, same as the word for *wind*.
And spirits are quite as unpredictable
As wind. None to know what next its game.

Perhaps to go on a rampage, whipping branches
About, defoliating autumnal trees;
Or flexing its fierceness and amputating limbs
A storm with a name, no longer anonymous breeze.

And televisionaries bloviate,
Stores exhaust of batteries and ply-;
People cautioned not to panic, panic
Imagining their lives go flying by.

Whether, in the end, it's a meteorological hell,
Or an illogical mindstorm, damage is wrought.
Be it cyclone or caressing breeze, wind,
The spirit, moves us and still we know it not.

Puzzles and Prizes

Nature steers me to puzzles and prizes.

Puzzle:
I come upon a seaside field
And find there, landbound, captive of grass,
A fisherman's wayward boat.
How? Why? That is the puzzle.

Prize:
A poem.
A poem about poets
A poem though that fails to parse the puzzle.

Poem:
One thinks of the Captain, O Captain, my Captain,
Steering his craft through leaves of grass,
Singing himself, singing himself,
When there's so much more to sing.

One thinks of the Belle ringing hollow to tell
Of her narrow fellow in the grass,
Parted grass as with a comb,
Her breathing tight and zero at the bone.

One thinks of the bard considering grass
To be but a nobleman's dying bed.

And then, in the end, one finds a friend
In the Savage Beauty of Maine,
Still young but given to know the ineffable spirit of grass;
Oh, at first she could not disregard
Those three long mountains, islands, wood
That bounded her and yet did not,
But when she learned to part the grass
(Part the leaves of grass with comb?)
Vincent believed she touched
The very heart of God.

Bard, Belle, Captain My Captain,
The Savage Beauty still can teach.

Pretenders

Our nation's first poet, a man of faith, spoke
Of the Spirit of Poetry. That is what Longfellow wrote.

As also a former Mainer, I would amend
To speak about poetry as not only Spirit
But also Sprite.

Spirit: the inspiring messenger voice of faith

Sprite: the playfully, always bubbling wraith
That brings us joy, engenders holy bliss.

Both Spirit and Sprite inhabit poetry done well,
As Longfellow did it; as we pretenders try.

Morning Gloam

I want to see shadows in early morning,
Shadows, nothing more.
No bright discernings, no colors, not yet,
Ne'er a random ray of light, for when there is light,
Light at all, there is color
And when there is color, it's late.
My sustaining time is the not-still dark
But not-yet-bright.
Gloam, let me call it, the gloaming of morn
Let my mind awake in monochrome.

A Simple Prayer

Dear God,

You know what I *can* be;
You know what you *want me* to be;
I know what I'd *like* to be.
But most of all I know
It's easiest to stay what I am.

May your will be done.

Mirrors

It is not enough to be hearers of God
We must, best we can, become Mirrors of God.